Thea Feldman

KINGFISHER

First published 2012 by Kingfisher
an imprint of Macmillan Children's Books
a division of Macmillan Publishers Limited
20 New Wharf Road, London N1 9RR
Basingstoke and Oxford
Associated companies throughout the world
www.panmacmillan.com

Series editor: Heather Morris
Literacy consultant: Hilary Horton

ISBN: 978-0-7534-3316-4
Copyright © Macmillan Publishers Ltd 2012

9 8 7 6 5 4 3 2 1

1TR/1011/WKT/UNTD/105MA

A CIP catalogue record for this book is available from the British Library.

Printed in China

Picture credits

The Publisher would like to thank the following for permission to reproduce their material. Every care has
been taken to trace copyright holders. However, if there have been unintentional omissions or failure to trace
copyright holders, we apologize and will, if informed, endeavour to make corrections in any future edition.
Top = t; Bottom = b; Centre = c; Left = l; Right = r
Cover Shutterstock; Pages 3 Frank Lane Picture Agency (FLPA)/Mitsuako Iwago/Minden; 4 Shutterstock/
Tom Pingel; 5 Shutterstock/Dmitry Pichugin; 6 Shutterstock/Imageman; 7 FLPA/Paul Sawer;
8–9 Shutterstock/Albie Venter; 9 FLPA/Katherine Feng/Minden; 10–11 Shutterstock/Theodore Mattas;
12 FLPA/Hiroya Minakuchi/Minden; 13 Shutterstock/Sergey Uryadnikov; 14 FLPA/Konrad Wothe/Minden;
15 FLPA/Paul Sawer; 16–17 Photolibrary/Peter Arnold Images; 17t Photolibrary/Martin Ruegner;
18 FLPA/Sunset; 19 Shutterstock/Rufous; 20 Alamy/Ashley Cooper; 21 Shutterstock/Ljupco Smokovski;
22 Shutterstock/Pakhnyushcha; 23 FLPA/David Tipling; 24–25 Shutterstock/Kletr; 24b Photolibrary/
Animals Animals; 26 Photolibrary/Imagebroker; 27 Photolibrary/Animals Animals; 28 FLPA/Michael
& Patricia Fogden/Minden Pictures; 29 Shutterstock/Imagestalk; 30–31 Corbis/Ocean.

Look!

This dog has babies.

A baby dog is a **puppy**.

Every animal begins life
as a baby.

A baby cat is a **kitten**.

A baby cow is a **calf**.

A baby rabbit is a kitten, too.

A baby deer is a **fawn**.

Some baby animals
are big.

baby elephant

Some baby animals are small.

baby panda

Some baby animals are
born at the same time
as their brothers and sisters.

Lion **cubs** are born together.

Baby killer whales
are born one at a time.

So are baby orang-utans.

How are all these
baby animals alike?

They all are cared for
by their mothers.

Some baby animals are fed
by their mothers.

These **piglets** get milk
from their mother.

Baby animals need
safe places to stay.

A mother will find a place.

A baby kangaroo is safe
in its mother's pouch.

Do you see how
a baby crocodile stays safe?

It takes a ride
in its mother's mouth.

A baby crocodile begins life inside an egg.

Baby birds come from eggs too.

Crack!

When it is ready to be born,
a baby chicken **hatches**
out of the egg.

Ducklings hatch from eggs too.

So does a penguin **chick**.

Some baby animals do not need to be cared for by their mothers.

Baby spiders do not need care.

Baby snakes do not need care.

When baby turtles hatch,
they are ready to go.

So are baby lizards.

Baby frogs are called **tadpoles**.

Do tadpoles look like
grown-up frogs?

No.

A grown-up frog looks like this.

Every animal begins
life as a baby.

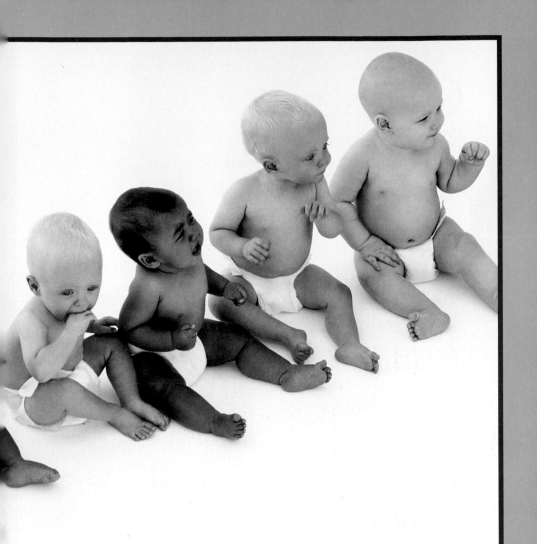

You did too!

Glossary

calf a baby cow, elephant or whale, or baby of some other kinds of large animals

chick a baby chicken or penguin, or baby of some other kinds of birds

cub a baby lion or bear, or baby of some other kinds of meat-eating animals

duckling a baby duck

fawn a baby deer

hatches breaks out of an egg and is born

kitten a baby cat, or sometimes a baby rabbit

piglet a baby pig

puppy a baby dog

tadpole a baby frog